# WHY DOES MY BODY DO THAT?

# STOMACH GROWL

by Rachel Rose

Consultant: Beth Gambro
Reading Specialist, Yorkville, Illinois

Minneapolis, Minnesota

# Teaching Tips

## Before Reading

- Look at the cover of the book. Discuss the picture and the title.
- Ask readers to brainstorm a list of what they already know about stomachs growling. What can they expect to see in this book?
- Go on a picture walk, looking through the pictures to discuss vocabulary and make predictions about the text.

## During Reading

- Read for purpose. Encourage readers to think about stomachs growling as they are reading.
- Ask readers to look for the details of the book. What are they learning about the body and how the stomach growls?
- If readers encounter an unknown word, ask them to look at the sounds in the word. Then, ask them to look at the rest of the page. Are there any clues to help them understand?

## After Reading

- Encourage readers to pick a buddy and reread the book together.
- Ask readers to name two things that can cause stomachs to growl. Find the pages that tell about these things.
- Ask readers to write or draw something they learned about stomach growls.

**Credits:** Cover and title page, © szefei/Shutterstock and © Zyn Chakrapong/Shutterstock; 3, © FatCamera/iStock; 5, © AaronAmat/Getty Images and © Thi Soares/iStock; 6–7, © FatCamera/iStock; 8, © fcafotodigital/iStock; 9, © magicmine/iStock; 11, © Trong Nguyen/Shutterstock and © Makistock/Shutterstock; 12–13, © A3pfamily/Shutterstock; 15, © Anatoliy Karlyuk/Shutterstock; 17, © fstop123/iStock; 19, © Rawpixel/iStock; 20–21, © Wavebreakmedia/iStock; 22, © Tetiana Lazunova/iStock; 23TL, © prill/iStock; 23TR, © SDI Productions/iStock; 23BL, © SDI Productions/iStock; 23BC, © HeidiFrerichs/iStock; and 23BR, © yodiyim/iStock.

Library of Congress Cataloging-in-Publication Data is available at www.loc.gov or upon request from the publisher.

ISBN: 978-1-63691-822-8 (hardcover)
ISBN: 978-1-63691-829-7 (paperback)
ISBN: 978-1-63691-836-5 (ebook)

Copyright © 2023 Bearport Publishing Company. All rights reserved. No part of this publication may be reproduced in whole or in part, stored in any retrieval system, or transmitted in any form or by any means, electronic, mechanical, photocopying, recording, or otherwise, without written permission from the publisher.

For more information, write to Bearport Publishing, 5357 Penn Avenue South, Minneapolis, MN 55419. Printed in the United States of America.

# Contents

**A Strange Sound** .................. 4

See It Happen ........................... 22

Glossary ................................. 23

Index .................................... 24

Read More ............................... 24

Learn More Online ....................... 24

About the Author ........................ 24

# A Strange Sound

It is almost time for lunch.

I am very hungry.

My **stomach** makes a strange sound.

*Growl!*

Why does my body do that?

There may be many stomachs growling in your class.

It happens to everyone!

But how does it work?

It often starts when you are hungry.

When your belly is empty, **muscles** there start to **squeeze**.

They are getting ready for food to come.

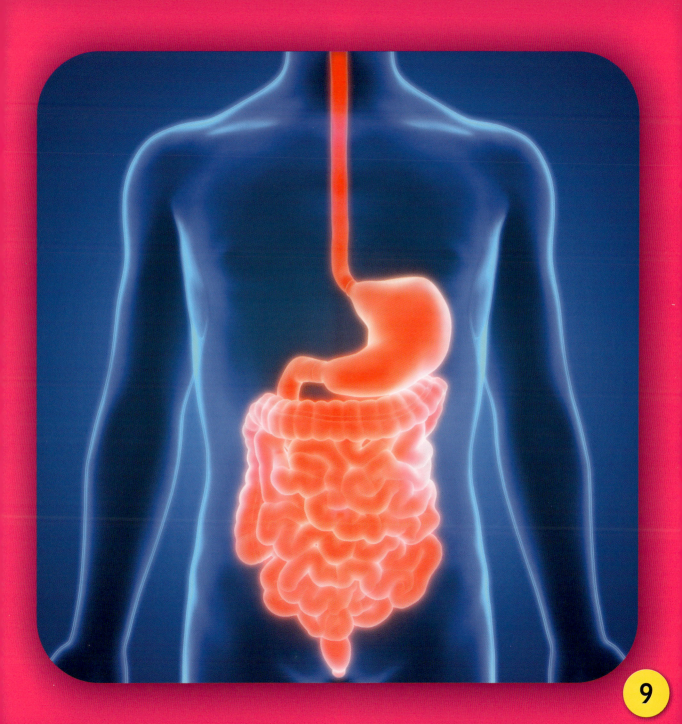

But there is no food in there.

It is mostly **gases** and air.

The gases and air are squeezed.

This makes your stomach growl.

When you finally get food, the growling does not stop.

It can happen after you eat, too!

The same muscles squeeze to break down food.

Now, they make your stomach gurgle.

This is often quieter than when there is no food.

How can you stop loud stomach growls?

Sometimes, drinking water can help.

It might work to eat a snack.

Some people feel shy if their stomachs growl.

Others think it is funny!

What do you think when it happens to you?

It is okay if your stomach growls.

In fact, it is very **healthy**.

Your body is doing what it is supposed to do!

*Ruuumble!*

21

# See It Happen

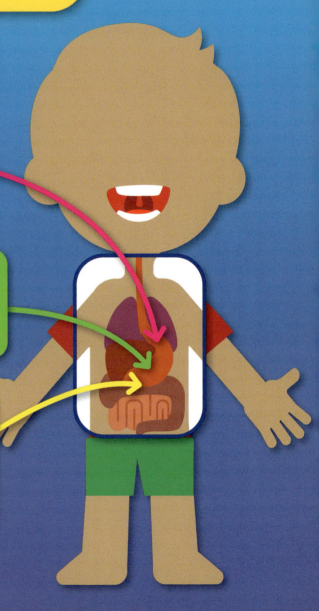

When you are hungry, the muscles in your belly start to squeeze.

There are only gases and air in your belly. The squeezing makes loud sounds.

You can make sounds after eating, too! It happens when muscles squish food to break it down.

# Glossary

**gases** things like air with no shape

**healthy** not ill

**muscles** parts of the body that move and help you do things

**squeeze** to press tightly

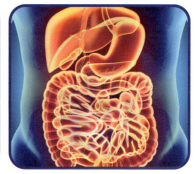

**stomach** the part of the body that breaks down food

# Index

**air** 10, 22
**food** 8, 10, 12, 14, 22
**gases** 10, 22
**healthy** 20

**muscles** 8, 14, 22
**snack** 16
**water** 16

# Read More

**Hughes, Sloane.** *My Stomach (What's Inside Me?).* Minneapolis: Bearport Publishing Company, 2022.

**Schuh, Mari.** *Dax's Dependable Digestive System (Let's Look at Body Systems!).* Minneapolis: Jump!, Inc., 2022

# Learn More Online

1. Go to **www.factsurfer.com** or scan the QR code below.
2. Enter "**Stomach Growl**" into the search box.
3. Click on the cover of this book to see a list of websites.

# About the Author

Rachel Rose lives in California. When her stomach growls, she thinks it's funny!